The Great Peshtigo Fire

The Great PESHTIGO FIRE

Stories and Science
from America's Deadliest Firestorm

SCOTT KNICKELBINE

Wisconsin Historical Society Press

Published by the Wisconsin Historical Society Press
Publishers since 1855

© 2012 by the State Historical Society of Wisconsin

wisconsinhistory.org

Printed in the United States of America
Designed by Shawn Biner, Biner Design

16 15 14 13 12   1 2 3 4 5
Library of Congress Cataloging-in-Publication Data
Knickelbine, Scott.
   The great Peshtigo fire: stories and science from America's deadliest firestorm / Scott Knickelbine.
      p. cm.
   Includes bibliographical references and index.
   ISBN 978-0-87020-499-9 (pbk. : alk. paper) 1. Peshtigo (Wis.)—History—19th century—Juvenile literature. 2. Peshtigo Region (Wis.) —History—19th century—Juvenile literature. 3. Fires—Wisconsin—Peshtigo—History—19th century—Juvenile literature. 4. Whirlwinds—Wisconsin—Peshtigo—History—19th century—Juvenile literature. 5. Forest fires—Wisconsin—Peshtigo Region—History—19th century—Juvenile literature. 6. Fires—Social aspects—Wisconsin—Peshtigo—History—19th century—Juvenile literature. I. Title.
   F589.P48K58 2012
   977.5'33—dc23
                              2012009085

This book is dedicated to my wife, Jean,

who did so much of the work on it.

—SLK

Contents

PESHTIGO RIVER

Chapter 1
A Tornado of Fire

The people of the little woodland village of Peshtigo, Wisconsin, had lived through many kinds of storms. Rainstorms that made the creeks and rivers flow over their banks. Windstorms that ripped trees from their roots. Hailstorms that crushed their crops with chunks of ice. Snowstorms that piled snow up over the windows and doors of their log cabins.

But they had never seen a storm made of fire.

Yet now, on this awful night, October 8, 1871, a firestorm was rushing down on them. It was a blazing tornado. And it was moving as fast as a freight train. Everything in the fire's path burst into flame—the forest, crops, and homes. Though Peshtigo had

Photo by Cheryl Morrill

This fire tornado photographed in Maine in 2004 was a small version of the one that destroyed Peshtigo in 1871.

Mapping Specialists, LTD

The fires of 1871 affected the entire northeastern part of Wisconsin.

Photo courtesy of the Image Bureau of Land Management, Idaho Office, Lower Snake River District, Four River Field Office

lived through many kinds of storms, hundreds of its people would not live through this night.

By the time the sun came up, a huge part of northeastern Wisconsin and northern Michigan was in ashes. Peshtigo and 11 other towns were wiped out. As many as 2,500 people were dead. So many died that even today, we don't know all their names.

In this photo taken in Idaho in 2008, smoke lingers after a fire has raged through the forest.

Photo courtesy of the Library of Congress Prints and Photographs Division, Washington, DC

This picture, made from five photographs, shows how much of Chicago was destroyed by the fire that blazed the same night as the Peshtigo Fire.

The Peshtigo Fire is remembered as one of the deadliest fires in US history. It killed even more people than the Great Chicago Fire, which happened on the same night. But Chicago was a big city with many newspapers and **telegraph** offices. The news of the fire that burned hundreds of Chicago's businesses, homes, and factories spread quickly. The Great Chicago Fire became famous. But Peshtigo was a far-off **frontier** settlement. The fire cut it off from the rest of the world. Even though the Peshtigo Fire killed many more people, it took much longer for others to find out about it. Today, experts who study fires know all about Peshtigo. But most people outside of Wisconsin have never heard of it.

How did the Peshtigo Fire start? How could there be a storm of fire? What did people do to try to stay alive? And how did this disaster change the lives of the people of Wisconsin, and all Americans? This book will answer those questions.

telegraph (**tel** uh graf): a form of communication that uses electrical signals sent through wires • **frontier** (fruhn **teer**): land at the edge of a settled area where people are just starting to build

How Can Fire Make a Storm?

The swirling winds caused by firestorms can create fire tornadoes, like this one at Morine Creek in Oregon in 2008.

To know what makes a firestorm, you need to remember two things. First, fires need **oxygen**—the same gas we breathe—to burn. Second, hot air rises and cold air sinks.

When a fire burns, hot air around the flame goes up. Then cool air below the flame rushes in to take its place. This cool air has fresh oxygen, which helps the fire keep burning. As this cool air heats up, it rises, too. Then more cool air comes in.

The bigger a fire gets, the more hot air it sends up and the more cool air it sucks in. Very large fires can pull in so much air that they can cause winds of 60 to 80 miles an hour. These high winds give the fire so much oxygen that it burns very hot—hot enough to melt metal and make everything around it burst into flame. The high heat makes even more air rise, and the winds of the firestorm become even stronger.

Because the firestorm is drawing in winds from all directions, the winds can meet and spin around each other, causing a fire tornado. Fire tornadoes combine damaging winds and blazing hot flames. Fire tornadoes destroy things in their path and spread the fire very quickly.

oxygen (**ok** suh juhn): one of the gases that make up the air we breathe

Chapter 2

Burning to Build, Building to Burn

In the North Woods of Wisconsin, it seemed like something was always burning.

People everywhere have always used fire to warm their homes and cook their food. Native people used fire to clear away brush and to drive hunted animals out of the forest. They even used smoke to send messages to people far away.

Fire was also a useful tool. For the thousands of people who settled in the forests of Wisconsin in the late 1800s, fire helped them turn a wild woodland into farms and towns. Fire cleared a path for railroad tracks and made the steam that ran the trains.

Photo courtesy of the Bureau of Land Management, Oregon Office

Most of northern Wisconsin was once completely covered by trees.

"Trees, Trees Everywhere"

Father Peter Pernin was a priest in Peshtigo. He described northeastern Wisconsin in the 1870s as "a country covered with dense forests. . . . With the exception of isolated spots where the trees have been cut down and burned, all is a wild but **majestic** forest. Trees, trees everywhere, nothing else but trees as far as you can travel from the bay, either towards the north or west."

This picture, taken in the Nicolet National Forest in northern Wisconsin, shows the kinds of trees that once covered the state.

The more people who moved to the forests of Wisconsin, the more fires they built. And more fires set **deliberately** meant a greater chance that some of those fires could get out of control.

majestic (muh **jes** tik): very big and awesome
deliberately (dee **lib** ur uht lee): on purpose

A Growing Nation Needs Wood

In 1871, the United States was only 95 years old. But the country was growing fast.

In the late 1800s, people were coming to America from all over the world. Some moved to the frontier to start farms or

Before the railroads came to Wisconsin, supplies had to be carried through the thick woods in horse-drawn wagons.

WHi Image ID 60232

ranches. Much of the good farmland in the East was already claimed. And many of the large old trees in the eastern forests had been cut down. So many of the new settlers kept moving west, looking for **unclaimed** land and uncut forests.

Millions of other **immigrants** were flocking to big cities like Chicago and New York. They came to get jobs in the factories, or to start stores, hotels, or other businesses. Even if

unclaimed: not said to belong to anyone • **immigrants** (**im** uh gruhnts): people who come into a country or region to live there

they planned to own a farm of their own, many immigrants needed to live in the city for a while to earn money to buy land. American cities grew quickly at this time.

These new immigrants needed places to live. They needed to build barns and stables, shops and factories. The fastest and cheapest way to put up a building was to make it out of wood. People knew that wood houses caught fire more easily than those made of brick and stone. But brick and stone were expensive to haul out to the new settlements. And the forests of the western Great Lakes states had plenty of wood. For these reasons, most of the towns and cities on the western frontier were built of wood.

People needed wood for other things, too. Everyday items like tables and chairs, bowls and buckets, broom handles and barrels were made from wood. People needed wood to make tools like axe handles, plows, and yokes. As the country got bigger, so did its hunger for wood.

WHi Image ID 41751

In the late 1800s, millions of immigrants came from Europe to find a new home in the United States.

WHi Image ID 62557

WISCONSIN.

What it offers to the Immigrant.

AN OFFICIAL REPORT

PUBLISHED BY THE

STATE BOARD OF IMMIGRATION OF WISCONSIN.

BOARD OF COMMISSIONERS:

This booklet was printed in 1879 to encourage new immigrants to settle in Wisconsin.

Logging

Wisconsin was a good place to get the wood people needed. It may seem hard to imagine now, but the whole northern half of Wisconsin was once one large, thick forest. It was covered with huge, very old trees. It was said that a squirrel could jump its way from tree to tree all the way from northern Michigan to Minnesota without ever touching the ground!

A team of horses draw a big load of wood through a Wisconsin forest.

By the 1870s there were thousands of men working at logging camps across the North Woods. These loggers cut down tens of thousands of huge pine trees every year. As the loggers cut all the trees in one place, they left behind big piles of "slash," the branches and sticks that they trimmed off the tree trunks. They also left behind the shrubs and small plants that grew beneath the pines. As all this waste wood dried out, it burned very easily. Sometimes the loggers burned the brush themselves, if it was in their way.

WHi Image ID 2196

Even in 1929, when this photo was taken, people traveling in northern Wisconsin could expect a long, bumpy ride through the woods.

Photo courtesy of the Bureau of Land Management, California Office

Loggers often burned the branches that were left over after they cut the trees from an area. Here, branches burn in a 2008 fire in California.

WHi Image ID 2875

Lumber mills were started all over Wisconsin to turn those trees into boards for building. The towns around Peshtigo had many lumber mills. Peshtigo also had a big factory that made buckets and broom handles and other things from wood. By 1870, almost 2,000 people had moved to Peshtigo to work in the logging camps, mills, and factories. All these people needed places to live, so they built homes out of the one thing they had plenty of: wood. And so towns like Peshtigo, Oconto, and Marinette grew quickly. And the forests gave way to streets lined with wooden houses.

Loggers move floating logs down the Peshtigo River in the early 1900s.

Photo by Jean Knickelbine

A sign from the Peshtigo Lumber Company, which gave jobs to hundreds of men before the fire

New York Public Library's Digital Library, Digital ID C90F384_002F

A picture showing one of Peshtigo's wooden products factories, taken four years before the fire

Farming

Once the loggers had removed most of the timber, the land was not much use to the logging companies and railroads that owned it. So they sold this "cutover" land to farmers. Some of these settlers hoped to grow crops like oats, wheat, and barley. Others planned to grow hay and clover to feed cows, sheep, and goats. In the late 1800s, hundreds of thousands of settlers came to Wisconsin to start farms.

But before they could start to plow the soil, the farmers had to get rid of the huge tree stumps the loggers had left behind. They had to clear away the thick bushes that grew between the trees and the thick grasses and weeds that covered the clearings. The fastest way to do this was by burning them. It often took more than a year to clear land for farming, and the settlers often had fires going night and day.

WHi Image ID 25050

A Wisconsin farm in 1873. Farmers often built on fields that were once covered with trees.

WHi Image ID 31824

Once all the trees were cut down in an area, farmers would remove the stumps so they could plow the fields.

Railroads

Railroads helped Wisconsin grow very fast. Trains carried logs, lumber, iron ore, and farm goods from forests and farms to big cities like Chicago. On the way back, they brought the tools, clothing, and other supplies the settlers needed. The railroads also brought more settlers.

Railroads and logging went hand in hand. Railroads made it easier to move logs and lumber out of the forest even in winter, so

WHi Image ID 5049

Men building a railroad track through a Wisconsin forest

WHi Image ID 24557

Horses pull a railroad engine over the land to a new railroad in Richland Center, Wisconsin, in 1876.

the loggers could cut year-round. It cost less to ship the lumber by train, so more people in cities like Chicago could afford it. As wood became cheaper, people wanted more of it. Railroads turned logging into an even larger **industry** in Wisconsin.

Railroads were so important that many people could not wait to bring them farther and farther north. The crews that built the railroad tracks often cut the trees in their path and burned them in huge fires.

These early trains ran on steam. In the train engines, wood or coal fires heated great tanks of water. As the water turned to steam, it pushed on **pistons** that turned the wheels of the engine and made it go. The fires in the engines burned so hot they threw sparks out their great smokestacks. Dry brush along the railroad tracks often caught fire as the trains roared past.

industry: the production of all kinds of goods, especially in factories or plants, or a kind of business that makes a particular product • **pistons**: round pieces of metal that are powered by the force of hot gases, steam, or liquid to make the parts of an engine move

Industry

Along with logging and farming, Wisconsin settlers started many new industries. Sawmills turned logs into planks and boards. The mills in Peshtigo turned out 50 million **board feet** of lumber every year. Peshtigo's woodenware factory was the biggest in the world at the time. Factory workers made hundreds of pails, tubs, broom and axe handles, and other goods.

A picture of the Peshtigo sawmill taken in 1867. The mill turned logs into boards and planks.

New York Public Library's Digital Library; Digital ID G90F384_001F

board feet: a way to measure wood that has been cut into boards. One board foot is the amount of wood in a board that is one foot wide, one foot long, and one inch thick.

Workplaces like the woodenware factory often used **steam-driven** equipment, so they too had fires burning to heat water. They also made sawdust—tons of it. There was no place to put the sawdust, so the factories just let it pile up in big hills or spread it over the streets. Sawdust burns very easily. In fact, if there's enough sawdust in the air on a hot, dry day, it can burst into flame all by itself!

There were also **foundries** that made iron goods that loggers, farmers, and factories needed, such as axe heads, barrel hoops, chain links, and more. These foundries built very hot coal or charcoal fires that melted iron so that it could be formed into different shapes. Sparks often flew from their smokestacks. Many other businesses, like charcoal factories and blacksmith shops, also used fire.

As the towns and farms around Peshtigo grew, the fires burned night and day. During dry weather in late summer and fall, fires often got out of control. Then they burned hundreds of acres of forest. People often lost their homes and farms to fire. Fire was a danger that the settlers in the North Woods both feared—and got used to.

Photo courtesy of Old World Wisconsin

A blacksmith creates objects by heating metal in fire until it's soft enough to be shaped with hand tools. In a frontier town like Peshtigo in the 1800s, blacksmiths would have made such items as latches, railings, nails, kettles, hoes, and plow blades.

steam-driven: getting its energy or motion from steam
foundries (**fown** dreez): factories where metal is melted and poured into molds to make useful objects

Chapter 3

The Forest in Flames

The late summer and early fall of 1871 were the driest any of the white settlers around Peshtigo had ever seen. There had not been much snow the winter before. Since July there had been almost no rain. Now the land was parched. Only a trickle of water ran in the little streams. Even the great swamps were dry. Some of the tall pines were so dry that they snapped in half when the wind blew hard. Farmers had to use wells to get water for their families and animals. But many of the wells were dry, too.

Low water in Peshtigo Harbor in 2008. The summer before the 1871 fire was one of the driest that people could remember.

Photo by Emmet Judziewicz, courtesy of the Wisconsin Department of Natural Resources

The Native people of the area were members of the **Menominee** Nation. They had lived in Wisconsin for hundreds of years. Even the Menominee elders could not remember such dry weather.

Menominee (muh **nah** muh nee): an Indian tribe living in northeastern Wisconsin

WHi Image ID 61832

Native Americans, like these Menominee Indians posing in ceremonial dress near Wausau, Wisconsin, relied on forest streams and wetlands for their food.

In the early spring of 1871, the maple trees gave little of the sap the Menominee people turned into sugar. When it came time to gather food, tribal members found only small, dried-out fruits and berries. They also had trouble harvesting wild rice. The marshes where the rice grew were so dry the Menominee could not float their canoes.

Many of the Menominee members were worried about having enough food for the winter. Some of them warned that big fires would be on the way.

WHi Image ID 30113

Ojibwe Indians pose with their canoes in this 1898 photo.

One of the settlers, Abram Place, was married to a woman from another northern Wisconsin Indian Nation, the **Ojibwe**. Her relatives warned the family a disaster was coming. Abram didn't want the fire coming up to his home. He went out and plowed up all the land around his house. He plowed under anything that could burn. But most of the farmers did not protect themselves this way.

Ojibwe (o **jib** way): One of the largest Indian tribes, living in many areas of the northern United States and southern Canada

Fires Everywhere

As summer turned to fall, the fires *did* come. Parts of the woods burned out of control, set off by a farmer's fire, or the sparks from a factory, or a strike of lightning. In the woods around the towns, some farms were lost to the fires. The settlers could put some of the smaller fires out. But many fires were just left to burn themselves out. Some people almost lost their lives in such fires.

Settlers in the 1800s had to fight forest fires with nothing but buckets and shovels. This picture of a crew fighting a forest fire was taken near Big Falls, Wisconsin, in 1910.

A painting of Father Peter Pernin, a Peshtigo priest who wrote one of the first histories of the fire

Father Peter Pernin went out one day to hunt in the woods. He brought along a boy from one of the country farms to help guide him. But they got lost, and it was dark before the boy's family found them. When Father Pernin and the boy tried to reach their rescuers, they found their way was blocked by fire. They turned around and saw the fire was burning behind them, too. The boy's family had to beat down the flames with tree branches to make a way for them to escape.

Smoke in the Air

With the fires burning all the time, the air in Peshtigo and Marinette was full of smoke. People walked the streets with handkerchiefs over their faces to block out the smoky air. Some days, the smoke was so bad that school was closed for the day. The smoke sometimes blocked the sun, so that people had to burn lamps to see even in the daytime.

The ships that traveled out on Lake Michigan's Green Bay had trouble finding their way to the harbors in Peshtigo and Marinette. The smoke was so thick that they could not see where they were going. They often blew their foghorns so they would not run into each other. Sometimes the ships had to stop where they were and wait for the smoke to clear.

Photo courtesy of the Image Bureau of Land Management, Oregon Office, Medford District. Filename: Meded2L-016.jpg

With so many fires burning, the air around Peshtigo was often filled with thick smoke. In this photo, the sun is barely peeking through the dark smoke coming from a fire in the state of Oregon.

Fire Strikes Peshtigo

On Sunday, September 24, a dangerous fire struck Peshtigo. The woods to the west of the town were burning. Sparks set a big mound of sawdust next to the woodenware factory on fire. The factory whistle blew in alarm. Hundreds of men from the town rushed to the factory and put out the fire with buckets of water from the river.

Seven miles away in Marinette on that same day, another fire came close to the town. Marinette's new volunteer fire company fought the fire all afternoon. Women tried to cover their homes with wet blankets to keep them from catching fire.

Both towns were saved that day, but people were frightened. Some of them packed their belongings and left. Others decided that they would bury things important to

them to protect them from fire. But most people in Peshtigo and Marinette went back to their everyday lives. So much of the forest around them had already burned. They thought they would be safe from any more fires. They also hoped it would rain soon.

Children gather in front of Peshtigo's schoolhouse in this engraving made from a photo taken before the 1871 fire.

WHi Image ID 2877

The Coming Storm

As September turned to October, the fires got worse, not better. Big grass fires in Minnesota began spreading into Wisconsin's North Woods. In fact, by early October fires were burning all the way from the Dakotas to northern Michigan.

Even worse, a huge **low-pressure cell** was forming in the west. This weather system was about to send high winds rushing right up along Green Bay, through Peshtigo and Marinette. And nothing makes a fire more deadly than high winds.

A US Department of Agriculture map of the storm that hit the Midwestern United States on October 8, 1871, shows the low-pressure cell that brought high winds to states including Wisconsin, Illinois, and Michigan.

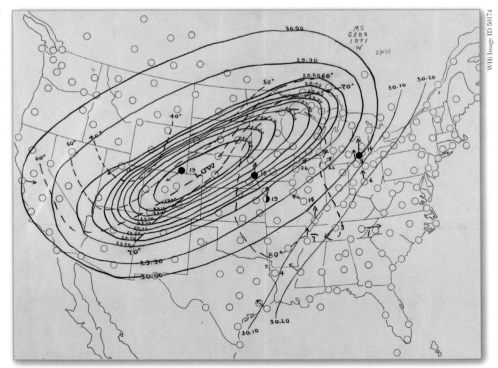

WHi Image ID 50174

low-pressure cell: an area where the air is not pressing down on the surface of the Earth as hard as it is in the areas around it

Low Pressure and Storms

Photo courtesy of NASA

A satellite photo of a low-pressure cell over the Midwestern United States, taken in 2003. The spiral shape of the clouds show how the winds around the cell spin in a counterclockwise direction.

Air pressure is how hard the air in a place is pushing down on the surface of the earth. A low-pressure cell forms in an area where the air pressure is lower than it is in the areas around it. In a low-pressure cell, the air rises and cools off, while air around the cell rushes in to replace it. When this happens, the air around the low-pressure cell spins counterclockwise. When the low-pressure area is very large, the spinning air around it can cause very high winds. The largest low-pressure systems are **hurricanes**. The winds spinning around a hurricane can reach more than 100 miles per hour!

air pressure: the force of the air in the atmosphere pushing down on the Earth
hurricane: a huge storm, often hundreds of miles across, that spins around a center point, called the eye

A Fire from Space?

Most experts think that the Peshtigo Fire was caused by many smaller fires that had been set by loggers and farmers. But some people think the fire had another cause—rocks falling from space.

A Leonid fireball meteor streaks through Earth's atmosphere in this 2001 photo. Some people think meteors might have caused the Peshtigo Fire, but most historians do not agree with this idea.

Some of the people who lived through the Peshtigo Fire said they saw great balls of fire flying through the sky. These strange lights landed with an earth-shaking roar. Some people think those flaming balls were **meteors**. Meteors are pieces of space rock that fall to the earth as "shooting stars." Could red-hot meteors have started the Peshtigo Fire?

Scientists who study forest fires say the shooting balls of flame some people saw that night were not meteors. They were large pieces of burning wood. The burning wood was carried high into the sky by the winds of the firestorm. These flaming chunks can fall far away from the fire. When they fall, it can look as though they have traveled from outer space, like a meteor.

meteors (**mee** tee orz): balls of rock and ice that burn up as they fall from outer space to Earth

Chapter 4
The Path of Death

The evening of Sunday, October 8, 1871, was a quiet one in Peshtigo. People went home from church. They were tired from fighting fires just days before. The low sky was cloudy and gray. The air was so full of smoke, it was hard to recognize someone standing just a few yards away. People were quiet from **exhaustion** and fear. Some people had a feeling that something terrible was about to happen.

Charlie Bakeman was a 10-year-old boy who lived on a farm outside of Peshtigo. His mother, Louisa, woke up that morning feeling that disaster was about to strike. She made Charlie's father bring all the cows into the barn and hitch the horses up to their wagon. Charlie and his brothers did not go hunting and fishing as they did every other Sunday. Instead, they had to spend time filling up all the barrels at the house with water from the well.

Before the Fire, mural panel painted by Luann Harff, Peshtigo Fire Museum; photo by Mark Fay

In the days before the fire, smoke from the grass fires burning throughout the countryside filled the air with gray smoke.

exhaustion (eg **zaws** chuhn): the feeling of being very tired or worn out

Charlie's mother couldn't say what made her feel afraid that something awful was about to happen. Charlie's father thought his wife's fears were completely **unreasonable**. Charlie was worn out from the day's chores and went to bed early.

Father Peter Pernin was busy in his backyard. He was burying gold and silver items from the church to protect them from fires. Next door, a group of women were having a tea party, laughing gaily. Loggers and mill workers drank, gambled, and fought at a **tavern** across the street. As the day grew darker, the skyline to the west was lit with a strange red glow. Close to dusk, the wind began to pick up. It blew stronger and stronger, carrying dust and ash from the earlier fires. The wind was also full of sparks.

At about 10 o'clock that night, a low rumbling sound over the **horizon** grew into a roar. People thought the noise sounded like a freight train or a huge rushing waterfall. The sound got louder and closer. Some families rushed into the street to see what was happening. Others locked their doors, hoping they would be safe inside.

Suddenly, big sheets of flame blew out of the forest. Everything in the path of the fire was instantly **consumed**. Some of the men in town rolled a big pumping engine down to the sawmill. The pumping engine was a machine that drew water from the river to spray on the fire. They had used it to fight many fires in the past. But in seconds the men saw that nothing they could do would stop this blaze. They ran for their lives.

unreasonable (uhn **ree** zuhn uh buhl): not showing good sense • **tavern**: a small business that sells food and drink • **horizon** (huh **ri** zuhn): the farthest edge of land that you can see • **consumed**: completely eaten up or destroyed

Photo by Cary Chancey, courtesy of the USDA, Forest Service Office

A picture taken in South Dakota in 2004 shows the damage that wildfires can cause.

Eight-year-old Fred Shephard woke up that night to the sound of someone banging on the window. People were shouting for his father, who was one of the men in charge of the Peshtigo Lumber Company. The town looked up to Fred's father as one of their leaders. They wanted him to tell them what to do about the fire. As his father rushed outside to take charge, Fred stayed in bed, scared nearly to death.

Painting by Mel Kishner, 1968, Wisconsin Historical Museum Object ID 1971.169.2

People in Peshtigo tried to escape the fire by running to the Peshtigo River. Hundreds of them never made it.

Soon the family's housekeeper came in and told Fred to get dressed as fast as he could. As he fumbled with his clothes, he looked out the window. All he could see to the west was flames. To the north, he could see the big Peshtigo Lumber Company **boardinghouse**. It was rocking back and forth in the grip of the high winds. Fred's father called to the rest of the family to leave the house by the back door and run to the river. Fred and the housekeeper struggled to get down to the river. Often the high wind blew them down to the ground. The air seemed too hot to breathe.

On the way to the river, Fred stopped for a moment in horror. He had forgotten all about Ned, the family dog! They had left Ned behind in the house. But it was too late to turn back now. He ran for the river.

boardinghouse: a business that rents out rooms for people to sleep in, usually for several weeks or months

Most of the people in town ran to the banks of the Peshtigo River. As they ran, dust and smoke blinded them. The wind blew them down. The sparks and flames blowing through the air set their hair and clothes on fire. Many died before they could reach the water.

When people did reach the edge of the river, they paused. Although the air was blazing hot, the water was chilly and cold. Many people could not swim. Some carried babies and small children in their arms. The water was already full of cows and horses. The animals were wildly **thrashing** in fear. But the wind was blowing the fire closer and closer to them. At last, the people began to jump in. They decided it was better to risk drowning than to be burned alive.

A drawing made after the fire shows people in Peshtigo seeking safety in the river.

WHi Image ID 3728

thrashing: moving around wildly

During the Fire, detail from mural panel painted by Luann Harff, Peshtigo Fire Museum; photo by Mark Fay

Horses and cattle often trampled on people as they struggled to reach the Peshtigo River.

Other people in Peshtigo thought they could outrun the fire. They threw their families in wagons and dashed madly out of town. People on both banks of the Peshtigo River tried to cross the town's single bridge. Each group thought they would be safe on the other side of the river! People from either side of the river collided in the middle, and the burning bridge fell down. People, horses, and wagons spilled into the river.

Some people tried to flee to a **clearing** south of town. They thought they might be safe where there were fewer trees to burn. But horses ran wild with fear, and wagons crashed into each other. As the path out of town narrowed, it became jammed with wagons. The firestorm quickly caught up to these wagons and burned everybody in them.

The people who looked for safety in the river found that they still had to fight for their lives. They were soaked to the skin. But if they kept their heads above water too long their hair would dry out and start to burn. Animals struggling to keep their heads above water accidentally pulled some people under. And the water was so chilly that some children and old people who had been saved from the fire ended up dying of cold.

clearing: a place in the middle of a forest or woods where there are no trees

As the townspeople looked up from the water, they saw that everything was on fire. Many of those who survived remembered that it looked like a tornado made of fire had swept through the town. Even the air high above them was on fire. As the hours wore on, people watched as everything they knew burned to the ground. Many of them thought that the world had come to an end.

"I Saw Nothing but Flames"

Father Pernin remembered his night in the Peshtigo River this way: "When turning my **gaze** from the river I chanced to look either to the right or left, before me or upwards, I saw nothing but flames; houses, trees, and the air itself were on fire. Above my head, as far as the eye could reach into space, alas! too **brilliantly** lighted, I saw nothing but immense volumes of flames . . . rolling one over the other with stormy violence."

During the Peshtigo Fire, the air itself seemed to be on fire. This picture was taken in Idaho in 2008.

Photo courtesy of the Bureau of Land Management, Idaho Office, Lower Snake River District, Four River Field Office

gaze: a long look
brilliantly (**bril** yuhnt lee): very brightly

Terror in the Woods

On the small farms in the woods around Peshtigo, even more people were dying. Some of these farm families tried to save themselves by running to the river, but others were too far away. Some people tried to save themselves by standing in the middle of a plowed field, but they were killed as sheets of flame moved through the air.

During the Fire, detail from mural panel painted by Luann Harff, Peshtigo Fire Museum; photo by Mark Fay

In the woods around Peshtigo, some people tried to escape the fire by running to town.

Other people crawled down into their wells, but many of them were killed by burning wood that fell into the wells. Still others died when the firestorm sucked all the air out of the well. Some were able to survive by lying in shallow streams or covering themselves with dirt or mud. Some found shelter from the fire behind a rock or small hill, while their families burned around them.

Charlie Bakeman and his brothers were just going to bed, bone tired from all the work they had done. They had been preparing their farm for the disaster their mother thought was coming. As they were falling into bed they heard a roaring noise outside. They looked out the window and saw that the sky was on fire. Then they heard their mother start to scream.

WHi Image ID 1881

People who were too far from water when the fire struck tried to find safety in the middle of open fields. They covered themselves with wet blankets to keep the hot sparks from setting them ablaze.

The family ran out to the barn and jumped into the lumber wagon, which they had left already hitched to the horses. They drove the horses at full speed to Charlie's uncle's house a mile away. Charlie looked around in terror. The wind was blowing so hard that it bent trees almost to the ground. The air was full of fire. Every now and then there was a blast in the air, like exploding gas.

What Is Flashover?

When wood and other plant materials get hot, they start to give off a gas that burns very easily. The hotter it gets, the more the gas builds up. Suddenly, this gas can burst into flame. When this happens, it looks like everything—even the air itself—is catching fire all at once. Firefighters call this a **flashover**. Many of the stories from people who lived through the Peshtigo Fire sound like they were seeing flashovers.

The Bakemans made it to Charlie's uncle's house, but it was clear the fire was catching up with them. Charlie's father stayed behind to help his uncle save his house, while Charlie's older brother, George, drove the wagon at full speed into Peshtigo. When they got to the river, they saw that a burning fence was in their way. Charlie and his older brother jumped through the flames. His mother grabbed the smaller children and threw them through the wall of fire, and then jumped through after them.

Other farmers also tried to outrun the fire. One of them, Charles Lamp, hitched up his team of horses, hurried his wife and children in the wagon, and tore down the narrow road to Peshtigo. But the fire caught up. Soon the Lamps were trying to put out their burning clothing. Then one of the horses lost its footing and fell. Charles Lamp jumped out of the wagon to help the horse up. When he turned around, he saw his whole family had burned. He was badly burned himself. But he saved his own life by lying flat in a nearby shallow creek.

flashover: the burst of flames caused when gases in the air suddenly catch on fire

Photo by Mark Fay

Charles Lamp saved himself from the fire by lying in this shallow creek in the woods near Peshtigo. His family died in the flames.

Survivors of that night of death told many stories like these. There seemed to be no place to run from the fire, no place to hide from it. Most of those who lived in the woods around Peshtigo never lived to see the next morning.

"The End of the World Is Coming!"

The tornado of fire moved on to the northwest. It cut a path along the Bay of Green Bay and struck the west side of Marinette.

Five-year-old Amelia **Desrochers** heard her mother scream in the night. "Charles," she cried to Amelia's father, "the end of the world is coming! Everything's on fire!" Her mother was standing by the tiny window in the little shack in Marinette where Amelia and her parents lived with Amelia's four brothers and sisters.

"Go to bed, go to bed," Amelia's father called back. "You're dreaming."

Amelia's mother begged him to come to the window. "Oh, Mother, you're right," he said. "Everything is on fire. I must be dreaming, too!"

But it was no dream. Already the little shack was lit up red inside from the flames that were getting nearer and nearer. "You'd better go to the river," Amelia's father said. "I'll stay home and try to save the home."

Amelia's mother quickly got the children dressed. They left in such a hurry that Amelia didn't even have time to put on her stockings. They ran down to the river, where a man at the bridge was telling people to get on a barge to escape. There wasn't enough

Desrochers: dee roh **shay**

Photo courtesy of the US Department of Agriculture

A wildfire lights up the night in this 2009 photo.

room on the barge for everyone, so only the women and children could get on board.

But even out in the water, they were not safe. The dry weather had left the river so low that the barge got stuck on the bottom. While the captain tried to get the barge going, it caught fire from the flames blowing from the shore. Some people thought all was lost. They jumped off the barge into the river, even though they couldn't swim. Many of them drowned.

But Amelia and her mother stayed on the boat. After many minutes the barge got going again and headed out into the Bay of Green Bay. Amelia stayed in the deckhouse of the barge in her mother's arms. When they were three miles out into the bay, she looked out the window of the deckhouse. Even so far from shore, red-hot ashes were drifting down from the sky, as thick as a winter snow.

The Chicago Fire

On the very same night as the Peshtigo Fire, the city of Chicago caught fire. Thousands of buildings burned over four square miles at the center of the city. Hundreds of people lost their lives, and 90,000 were left without a home. The fire was so hot that even the steel inside of brick buildings melted.

Really, it is not so strange that these two great fires happened on the same night. The Peshtigo and Chicago fires were just two of many big fires that swept the Midwest, from Minnesota to Michigan. The giant storm system caused high winds that fanned small blazes into huge fires.

After the Chicago fire of 1871, most of the downtown area lay in ruins. These buildings, which looked like skeletons after the fire, once stood along the city's "Bookseller's Row."

Library of Congress

Chapter 5
A Smoking Waste

When the survivors of the Peshtigo Fire dared to come out of the river the next morning, they could not believe what they saw. Their town was gone. Nearly every building had disappeared. People and animals were so badly burned that all that was left were little piles of ashes.

Everything they saw told them this had not been an ordinary fire. The bell from Father Pernin's church had actually melted in the heat. Strange holes were left in the ground where trees had burned right down to the ends of their roots. Patches of sand had gotten so hot they melted into glass. The tornado had tossed railroad cars around like a child's toys.

A brick smokestack is all that is left standing in this picture taken in Peshtigo after the fire.

After the Fire, detail from mural panel painted by Luann Harff, Peshtigo Fire Museum; photo by Mark Fay

Many survivors of the Peshtigo Fire had bad burns. They faced the cold morning with little clothing, often soaked to the skin.

But the survivors had little time to wonder about the strange fire. They were cold, wet, tired, and hungry. Many of them had been badly burned. All of them had breathed in so much hot smoke in the night that they couldn't stop coughing. There was nothing for them to do but try to keep living until help arrived. Many wandered around in a daze, calling out for lost family members.

Charlie Bakeman and his family pulled themselves out of the water. Charlie was surprised to see his mother holding a baby wrapped in a soggy blanket. She had found the baby in their dash to the river the night before. His mother scooped up the baby and protected it all night from the fire, along with her own children.

Now they were all freezing cold. They joined a group of survivors warming themselves near a pile of burning coal near what had once been the blacksmith's shop. Suddenly, a big man who worked at the sawmill grabbed the blanket with the baby in it. He wanted to steal the blanket for himself. He didn't know there was a baby inside!

Charlie's mother grabbed an iron rod that was sticking into the hot coals. The other end was glowing red hot. Waving the iron in front of her, she jumped after the man who had snatched the blanket. "You give that back!" she shouted. "That's mine!" The man handed the bundle back to Charlie's mother and ran off.

After the Fire, detail from mural panel painted by Luann Harff, Peshtigo Fire Museum; photo by Mark Fay

Charlie Bakeman's mother fought to save a baby she had found while running to the river to escape the fire.

The Fiddle That Survived Two Fires

In 1864, during the **Civil War**, **Union** troops marched through the **Confederate** state of Georgia. Union soldiers burned towns and farms as they went. Some Wisconsin soldiers fighting for the Union discovered a beautiful violin that had been buried to protect it from the flames. They gave it to their general, who later gave it to William Shephard, Fred Shephard's father. William Shephard was a fine fiddle player and an officer of the Peshtigo **Company**. Just before the Peshtigo Fire, Shephard buried the violin with some of his other things. After the fire, he came back to dig up the violin, which had stayed safe underground. Fifty years later, his son Fred still had that violin, which had survived two historic fires.

Fred Shephard waited near the river that morning. He shivered as he held onto his dog, Ned. Even though the family had left Ned behind, the dog had somehow managed to get out of the house and find Fred among all the people down at the river that night. Fred was tired, cold, and hungry. But he was grateful that at least he still had his pet.

Fred waited until his father had come back from looking at the ruins of Peshtigo. Fred begged his father to let him go look, too. But his father wouldn't let him go. He knew that the dead bodies of many of Fred's playmates were lying in the streets.

Up in Marinette the morning after the fire, the barge that carried people like Amelia Desrochers, her mother, and her brothers and sisters returned to the dock. Amelia and her family walked through the smoking

Civil War: the war between the Northern and Southern states (1861–1865)
Union (**yoo** nyuhn): the Northern states in the Civil War
Confederate (kuhn **fed** ur it): the Southern states in the Civil War
company: a group of soldiers

remains of the burned part of the city. When they saw that their shack had burned to the ground, they wondered if their father was still alive.

Finally they found him, along with Amelia's uncle, down at a **spring** not far away. The two men had moved all their furniture down to the spring. They had spent all night splashing the beds, chairs, and tables with water to keep them from burning. The furniture was saved, but Amelia's father had been blinded by the smoke. He heard his wife's voice, but he couldn't tell how many of his children were still alive. "I can't see," he said in a trembling voice. "Are they all safe?" He wouldn't calm down until he had grabbed the hand of each one of his children.

Photo courtesy of the US Bureau of Land Management, Idaho Office

A picture taken after a 2008 forest fire in Idaho, showing the damage left behind

spring: a place where fresh water comes up out of the ground

The Path of Destruction

The firestorm had swept from southwest of Peshtigo up through Marinette, destroying half of that city. Other fires around the firestorm burned an area from Lake Winnebago all the way up to northern Michigan. The fire was so intense that it crossed the waters of Green Bay and destroyed towns on the other side. All in all, more than 1,800 square miles of forest were burned.

Twelve towns and villages in the path of the fire were destroyed. Nobody knows how many were killed. Exact records of how many people lived in the towns were not kept, and nobody ever counted all the little farms spread out through the countryside. The bodies of the victims were often too burned to recognize, or even count.

Mapping Specialists, LTD

The firestorm swept from south of Oconto, northeast through Peshtigo and Marinette. Hot sparks and cinders blew across the Bay of Green Bay and spread the fire to Door County.

WHi Image ID 69692

A Native American family rests at their campsite in this 1925 photo. Nobody knows how many Menominee Indians were killed in the Peshtigo Fire.

No one knows how many Wisconsin Indians died in the fire either. The fire did not reach the **reservation** where most of the Menominee lived along the Wolf River near present-day Shawano. But a small band of 46 families lived along the Peshtigo River. There is no record of how many of them lived through the fire.

The best guess is that the fire killed at least 1,200 people, and maybe as many as 2,500. One thing is clear: more people died in the Peshtigo Fire than in any other US wildfire, before or since.

reservation (rez ur **vay** shuhn): an area of land set aside by the US government for an Indian tribe to live on

The fire also took a terrible toll on nature. Billions of trees—some of them hundreds of years old—were destroyed. Millions of animals living in the woods were killed. Dead fish covered the rivers. Thousands of birds fell to the ground. They had burned in midair as they tried to fly away. The smoke from the fire darkened the sun for many days after.

WHi Image ID 1859

A deer that probably died of its wounds after the fire lies amid the burned woods in the photo taken near Peshtigo after the fire.

Photo by John McColgan, courtesy of the US Department of Agriculture, US Forest Service

Wildlife around Peshtigo tried to find safety in the river, just as these elk did during a forest fire in Montana in 2000.

The Country Learns about the Fire

As bad as the Peshtigo Fire was, it took days before other people in Wisconsin found out about it. The telegraph wires that connected Peshtigo to the rest of the state were burned in the fire. The only way to get a message out about the disaster was to send it by steamship through the smoky waters from Peshtigo to Green Bay. The telegraph in Green Bay was still working.

It wasn't until two days after the fire that the news finally reached the home of Wisconsin governor Lucius Fairchild in Madison. But by that time, Governor Fairchild was no longer there. The news of the Great Chicago Fire reached Madison much sooner. Fairchild had taken a train to Chicago to find out how he could help the survivors there.

It took days before people in Wisconsin learned how bad the Peshtigo Fire had been. This article in the *Madison Daily Democrat* appeared five days after the fire.

Madison Daily Democrat, October 13, 1871

WHi Image ID 2828

WHi Image ID 47621

A photo taken in Peshtigo after the fire shows the only building left standing in the town.

But the governor's wife, Frances, was still in Madison. She got the message about the disaster at Peshtigo. She knew there was no time to lose. Although she wasn't the governor, Frances Fairchild took action! She stopped a train car loaded with food and supplies for Chicago and ordered that it be sent north instead.

Frances Fairchild called on people in Madison to quickly round up all the spare blankets they had. Then she had the blankets stuffed in the train car. She ordered the train to go to Green Bay, not Chicago. From there, the supplies could be carried by ship and wagon to the ruined towns. Because of her fast action, relief supplies got to the people of Peshtigo days earlier than they might have otherwise.

With Wisconsin governor Lucius Fairchild away in Chicago, his wife, Frances, took charge of sending relief supplies to Peshtigo.

WHi Image ID 2829

The remains of railroad tracks at Peshtigo after the fire. The iron wheels standing on the tracks were all that was left of the boxcars that once stood there.

By October 13, Governor Fairchild had gone to Green Bay himself to learn more about the disaster. From there he **appealed** to the people of his state to send help to the area. The news also got out to people in big eastern cities like New York and Boston.

appealed: made an important request

The Governor Calls for Help

Governor Lucius Fairchild's appeal to the people of Wisconsin was printed in several state newspapers. Here's what Governor Fairchild wrote on October 13, 1871:

To the People of Wisconsin:

*The accounts of the . . . **calamity** which has fallen upon the east and west shores of Green Bay have not been **exaggerated** . . . The loss of life has been very great. Even now it is feared that it is much greater than present accounts place it. It is known that at least one thousand persons have either burned, drowned or smothered. Of these deaths, six hundred or more at Peshtigo.*

BY TELEGRAPH.

THE GREAT FIRES

IN NORTHERN WISCONSIN.

Six Ccⁿⁱ Burned Over.

1,000 People Consumed,

3,000 RENDERED HOMELESS.

Starvation Staring Them in the Face.

PROCLAMATION BY GOVERNOR,

Calling for More Aid.

THE NORTHERN FIRES.
GREEN BAY, Oct. 13.
To the people of Wisconsin :
The accounts of the appalling calamity which has fallen upon the east and west shores of Green Bay, have not been exaggerated. The burned district comprises the counties of Oconto, Brown, Door and Ke-

Wisconsin State Journal, October 14, 1871

Governor Fairchild's call for help for the survivors of the Peshtigo Fire ran in many state newspapers, including the *Wisconsin State Journal*.

At first, people were too upset about the news from Chicago to pay much attention to a fire in Wisconsin. But when they learned how many more people had been killed in the Peshtigo Fire, they soon began to send help. They sent money and tons of food and clothing to Milwaukee and Green Bay. In fact, so much food and clothing arrived that the people in Milwaukee and Green Bay had trouble handling it all!

calamity (kah **lam** ih tee): a terrible disaster • **exaggerated** (eg **zaj** uh ray tid): made to sound bigger or more important than something really is

A Scene of Sadness

Even with all the aid rushing in, it took days and sometimes weeks for help to arrive. Most of the survivors in Peshtigo had been slowly taken to Marinette, where half the city remained unburned. There, hotels and houses were turned into hospitals, filled with injured and dying people. Survivors who had not been burned by the fire had damaged their lungs by breathing hot smoke. Peshtigo Harbor was a small village to the south and east of Peshtigo. And since it was out of the path of the fire, many survivors also went there.

Survivors out in the forest jammed into any buildings that were still standing. The Abram Place farm was still standing because his wife's Ojibwe relatives had warned the family to get ready for the fire.

Photo by Mark Fay

A bible that survived the fire was found in Peshtigo in 1995. The heat of the fire was so intense that it petrified the bible, turning it black and making it as hard as stone.

That's why the Place farm was one of the only farms that survived. Abram Place gave shelter to many other families who had lost their homes.

People who arrived from the outside world to help were shocked by what they saw. "We have had one of the most terrific fires that ever could be," one survivor wrote to his family from Peshtigo three days after the fire. "The City of Peshtigo is all in ashes and there is about nine or ten hundred persons burned. I have just got in from helping to bury them and Oh it is the worst sight I ever saw."

The fire had burned almost everything—even things people thought could not burn. All that was left were ashes, and even those were blowing away in the wind.

Chapter 6

Lessons of the Peshtigo Fire

The fires that swept through Peshtigo, Chicago, and so many other places in October 1871 shocked Americans. It made many people wonder if humans were being too careless about fire. People began to call for government to do more to prevent fires.

Fire Prevention

After the Chicago fire, the city passed new laws that required buildings to be more fireproof. Buildings also had to have ways for people to escape if the buildings caught on fire. These laws were **adopted** by many big cities. More and more towns also started fire departments or made them larger. They began to build systems of fire **hydrants** that made it easier for firefighters to get the water they needed to fight fires. Today, all US cities have fire codes—laws that tell people how to build homes and other buildings so they will be safer in a fire.

In some cities, "junior fire departments" were organized to give young people a chance to learn about firefighting and fire prevention. In this 1929 photo, a boy who's a member of the Chicago Junior Fire Department is unscrewing part of a fire hydrant.

adopted: made into a rule or law • **hydrants**: short standing metal pipes with caps on the top, which let firefighters get water from underground water pipes

Based on a real bear that survived a 1950 forest fire, Smokey Bear has become a symbol of forest fire prevention.

In 1925, President Calvin Coolidge declared the first week of October to be National Fire Prevention Week. The date was picked to remember the Great Chicago Fire. Today, it is a time for people to learn more about what causes fires and how to stop them from happening.

Americans also wanted to stop large forests from burning. In 1905, the US government created the US Forest Service. The job of the Forest Service was to protect forests and other wild lands from fire. Then, in 1910, a huge fire burned all the way from the Rocky Mountains to Minnesota. The fire became known as the Big Blowup. It didn't kill as many people as the Peshtigo Fire, but it was so big that it made people demand that more fires be prevented. Soon, fire prevention and control programs began to grow.

In 1950 a big fire raged in the Capitan Mountains in New Mexico. Afterward, firefighters found an orphaned bear cub up in a tree in an area where the fire had passed through. It had suffered burns and other injuries, but the little cub was rescued and its injuries were treated and bandaged. News about the bear spread throughout New Mexico and the rest of the United States. The bear became famous and was sent to Washington, DC, to live in the National Zoo. For the rest of its life the bear was called Smokey Bear, whose image became familiar to people everywhere as the symbol of forest fire prevention.

Photo by Jim Peaco, courtesy of the National Park Service

Some trees, like these lodgepole pines, need regular fires so that their seeds will grow.

Over the years, though, forest experts learned that stopping all fires wasn't such a good idea. It turned out that it was good for forests and prairies to have fires now and then. When dry grasses burn, they make way for new grass to grow. Some kinds of trees, like the lodgepole pine, won't even drop their seeds until after a fire.

There was another problem with stopping all fires. Without fire, dry, dead sticks and brush pile deeper and deeper in the forest. Then, when a fire finally does start, it is much larger and more dangerous. The Forest Service found out that it was better to have smaller fires that they could control than to have big ones they could not handle.

Today, the Forest Service tries to keep people from building homes too close to woods and fields that can burn. It also sometimes sets its own small and controllable fires to keep dry wood from building up.

Even so, every summer and fall there are some wildfires in America. A few of these get to be big enough to be called firestorms. Some even cause fire tornadoes, like the one that destroyed Peshtigo.

Setting Fires to Stop Fires

Photo courtesy of the US Fish and Wildlife Service, Branch of Fire Management, Sheldon Hart Mountains NWRC.

One way forest managers try to prevent deadly forest fires is by setting fires themselves. They wait until the wind and weather are just right, and they bring fire crews and equipment. Then they start a small fire to burn away dead wood and dry grasses. Before the fire gets too big, they put it out. But some people don't like the idea of the government starting fires.

These specially trained fire teams, called "hotshots," are setting small, controlled fires to burn off dry grasses and wood.

Back from the Ashes

Not long after the Peshtigo Fire, William Butler Ogden came to Peshtigo. Ogden owned most of the businesses in the town, and he announced he would rebuild the city. But it took him and the people living there years to rebuild the destroyed town. Many of the survivors never moved back. Many businesses never reopened.

WHi Image ID 22656

Another "bird's-eye" view of Peshtigo shows the rebuilt town, 10 years after the fire. Can you spot the differences between this picture and the one on the contents pages in the front of this book?

A new railroad was built after the fire, connecting Peshtigo to the harbor towns of Green Bay to the south and Marinette to the north.

The woodenware factory had supplied good jobs to many people. It was never rebuilt. Although the town became the city of Peshtigo in 1903, it was never the center of industry it had been before the fire.

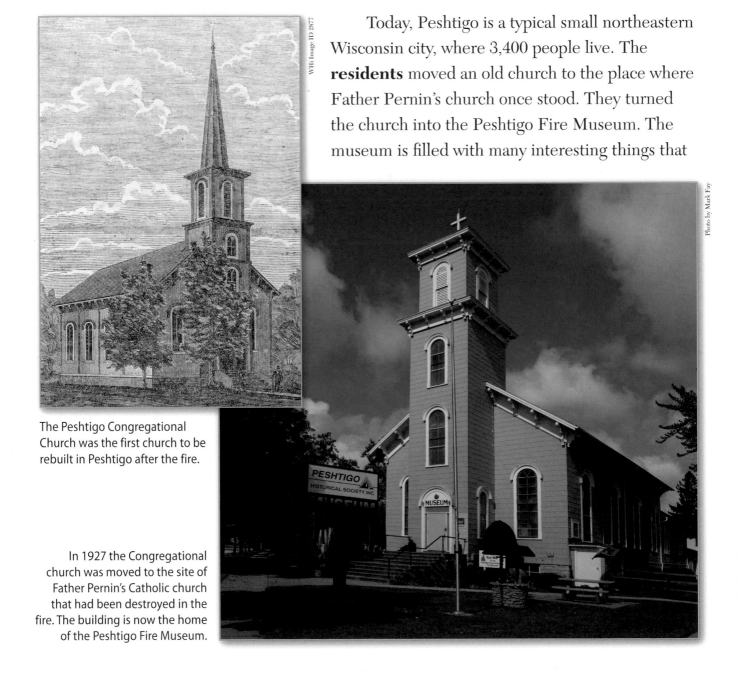

WHi Image ID 2877

Today, Peshtigo is a typical small northeastern Wisconsin city, where 3,400 people live. The **residents** moved an old church to the place where Father Pernin's church once stood. They turned the church into the Peshtigo Fire Museum. The museum is filled with many interesting things that

Photo by Mark Fay

The Peshtigo Congregational Church was the first church to be rebuilt in Peshtigo after the fire.

In 1927 the Congregational church was moved to the site of Father Pernin's Catholic church that had been destroyed in the fire. The building is now the home of the Peshtigo Fire Museum.

residents: people who live in a place

were saved from the fire. It has letters that were written by people who survived the fire. Many of the displays show what life was like in Peshtigo before it burned. The museum opens every spring, and it closes each year on October 8, the anniversary of the fire.

Close by the museum you can visit the Peshtigo Fire Cemetery, where many of those who died in the fire are buried. There is also a **mass grave**, where 350 people who could not be identified after the fire are buried.

The museum and the cemetery are both sad reminders of the Peshtigo Fire. They also remind us of what can happen when humans build without respecting the awesome power of fire.

Photo by Jean Knickelbine

A plaque marks the mass grave where unknown victims of the Peshtigo Fire lie buried.

mass grave: a place where many people are buried in the same hole in the ground

Time Line

1634 French explorer Jean Nicolet visits Wisconsin.

1717 First European settlement is started at Green Bay.

1827 Settlers begin building sawmills in the Peshtigo area.

1836 Wisconsin officially becomes a US Territory.

1848 Wisconsin becomes the 30th state.

1859 Town of Peshtigo is established.

1870 Population of Town of Peshtigo grows to 1,744.

1871 **July–September:** Many fires burn in northeastern Wisconsin as the state suffers the driest summer and fall on record.

September 24: The people of Peshtigo fight back a major blaze that starts when sparks blowing across the Peshtigo River start a pile of sawdust on fire.

October 1–7: Scattered forest and prairie fires are burning all the way from Lake Michigan to the Dakotas.

October 8: A firestorm sweeps from Peshtigo to Marinette, killing as many as 2,500 people and leaving 1.5 million acres of forest burned. It is the deadliest wildfire in American history.

October 8: A fire in Chicago kills 300 people and destroys hundreds of buildings.

1871 October 10: News of the Peshtigo Fire finally reaches the state capitol in Madison, but Governor Lucius Fairchild is in Chicago. His wife, Frances, takes charge of relief supplies for Peshtigo.

October 13: Governor Fairchild issues an appeal to the people of Wisconsin to help the survivors of the Peshtigo Fire.

1903 The City of Peshtigo is rebuilt and incorporated.

1905 Congress forms the US Forest Service to protect forests from fire.

1910 The Big Blowup destroys three million acres of forest and grassland and kills 78 firefighters.

1925 President Calvin Coolidge declares the week after the first Sunday in October National Fire Prevention Week.

1945 Firestorms caused by the World War II bombings of Dresden in Germany and Tokyo in Japan kill thousands of people. Information from the Peshtigo Fire is used by the Allies to start these firestorms.

1988 A fire started by lightning in Yellowstone National Park becomes the biggest single fire since the Peshtigo Fire.

Today More than 11,000 people from all 50 states and 22 foreign countries visit the Peshtigo Fire Museum.

Glossary

Pronunciation Key

a	c*a*t (kat), pl*ai*d (plad), h*a*lf (haf)
ah	f*a*ther (**fah** THur), h*ea*rt (hahrt)
air	c*a*rry (**kair** ee), b*ea*r (bair), wh*e*re (whair)
aw	*a*ll (awl), l*aw* (law), b*ough*t (bawt)
ay	s*ay* (say), br*ea*k (brayk), v*ei*n (vayn)
e	b*e*t (bet), s*ay*s (sez), d*ea*f (def)
ee	b*ee* (bee), t*ea*m (teem), f*ea*r (feer)
i	b*i*t (bit), w*o*men (**wim** uhn), b*ui*ld (bild)
I	*i*ce (Is), l*ie* (lI), sk*y* (skI)
o	h*o*t (hot), w*a*tch (wotch)
oh	*o*pen (**oh** puhn), s*ew* (soh)
oi	b*oi*l (boil), b*oy* (boi)
oo	p*oo*l (pool), m*o*ve (moov), sh*oe* (shoo)
or	*or*der (**or** dur), m*o*re (mor)
ou	h*ou*se (hous), n*ow* (nou)
u	g*oo*d (gud), sh*ou*ld (shud)
uh	c*u*p (kuhp), fl*oo*d (fluhd), b*u*tton (**buht** uhn)
ur	b*u*rn (burn), p*ea*rl (purl), b*i*rd (burd)
yoo	*u*se (yooz), f*ew* (fyoo), v*iew* (vyoo)
hw	*wh*at (hwuht), *wh*en (hwen)
TH	*th*at (THat), brea*the* (breeTH)
zh	mea*s*ure (**mezh** ur), gara*ge* (guh **razh**)

adopted: made into a rule or law

air pressure: the force of the air in the atmosphere pushing down on the Earth

appealed: made an important request

board feet: a way to measure wood that has been cut into boards. One board foot is the amount of wood in a board that is one foot wide, one foot long, and one inch thick.

boardinghouse: a business that rents out rooms for people to sleep in, usually for several weeks or months

brilliantly (**bril** yuhnt lee): very brightly

calamity (kah **lam** ih tee): a terrible disaster

Civil War: the war between the Northern and Southern states (1861–1865)

clearing: a place in the middle of a forest or woods where there are no trees

company: a group of soldiers

Confederate (kuhn **fed** ur it): the Southern states in the Civil War

consumed: completely eaten up or destroyed

deliberately (dee **lib** ur uht lee): on purpose

exaggerated (eg **zaj** uh ray tid): made to sound bigger or more important than something really is

exhaustion (eg **zaws** chuhn): the feeling of being very tired or worn out

flashover: the burst of flames caused when gases in the air suddenly catch on fire

foundries (**fown** dreez): factories where metal is melted and poured into molds to make useful objects

frontier (fruhn **teer**): land at the edge of a settled area where people are just starting to build

gaze: a long look

horizon (huh **ri** zuhn): the farthest edge of land that you can see

hurricane: a huge storm, often hundreds of miles across, that spins around a center point, called the eye

hydrants: short standing metal pipes with caps on the top, which let firefighters get water from underground water pipes

immigrants (**im** uh gruhnts): people who come into a country or region to live there

industry: the production of all kinds of goods, especially in factories or plants, or a kind of business that makes a particular product

low-pressure cell: an area where the air is not pressing down on the surface of the Earth as hard as it is in the areas around it

majestic (muh **jes** tik): very big and awesome

mass grave: a place where many people are buried in the same hole in the ground

Menominee (muh **nah** muh nee): an Indian tribe living in northeastern Wisconsin

meteors (**mee** tee urz): Balls of rock and ice that burn up as they fall from outer space to Earth

Ojibwe (o **jib** way): One of the largest Indian tribes, living in many areas of the northern United States and southern Canada.

oxygen (**ok** suh juhn): one of the gases that make up the air we breathe

pistons: round pieces of metal that are powered by the force of hot gasses, steam, or liquid to make the parts of an engine move

reservation (rez ur **vay** shuhn): an area of land set aside by the US government for an Indian tribe to live on

residents: people who live in a place

spring: a place where fresh water comes up out of the ground

steam-driven: getting its energy or motion from steam

tavern: a small business that sells food and drink

telegraph (**tel** uh graf): a form of communication that uses electrical signals sent through wires

thrashing: moving around wildly

unclaimed: not said to belong to anyone

Union (**yoo** nyuhn): the Northern states in the Civil War

unreasonable (uhn **ree** zuhn uh buhl): not showing good sense

To Learn More

Costain, Meredith. *Devouring Flames: The Story of Forest Fires.* New York: National Geographic Children's Books, 2006.

Guess, Denise, and William Lutz. *Firestorm at Peshtigo.* New York: Henry Holt, 2003.

Murphy, Jim. *The Great Fire.* New York: Scholastic Paperbacks, 2006.

Pernin, Rev. Peter. *The Great Peshtigo Fire: An Eyewitness Account.* 2nd ed. Madison: Wisconsin Historical Society Press, 1999.

Wells, Robert. *Embers of October.* Peshtigo: Wisconsin Tales & Trails, 1973.

Chicago Historical Society and Northwestern University. "The Great Chicago Fire and the Web of Memory." www.chicagohs.org/fire

Hipke, Deana C. "The Great Peshtigo Fire of 1871." www.peshtigofire.info

Oconto County WIGenWeb Project. "The Great Peshtigo Fire." www.rootsweb.ancestry.com/~wioconto/Fire.htm

US Department of Agriculture. *SmokeyBear.com.* www.smokeybear.com/kids/default.asp?js=1

Wisconsin Electronic Reader. "The Great Fires of 1871 in the Northwest." www.library.wisc.edu/etext/wireader /WER0133.htm

Peshtigo Fire Museum, 400 Oconto Avenue, Peshtigo, WI 54157
715-582-3244
www.peshtigofire.info/museum.htm
Open May to October

Index

This index points you to the pages where you can read about persons, places, and ideas. If you do not find the word you are looking for, try to think of another word that means about the same thing.

When you see a page number in **bold** it means there is a picture on that page.

About the Author

Scott Knickelbine has been writing about Wisconsin history since 1978, when he was coauthor of the historical radio series *Neshota Sam.* He is the author of more than 40 books, most of them historical nonfiction works for young readers. His work has appeared in hundreds of newspapers and magazines, and he has written more than 600 how-to articles for the Internet. He was born in Manitowoc, Wisconsin, and received his bachelor's degree in journalism from the University of Minnesota in 1981.

Photo by Jean Knickelbine